¡SLIMED!

Contents

True *Slime* Stories

Written by Laura Hirschfield

Lungfish

Some animals eat slime.
Some walk on it.
Some fight with it.
This lungfish even sleeps in it!
Which would you rather do?

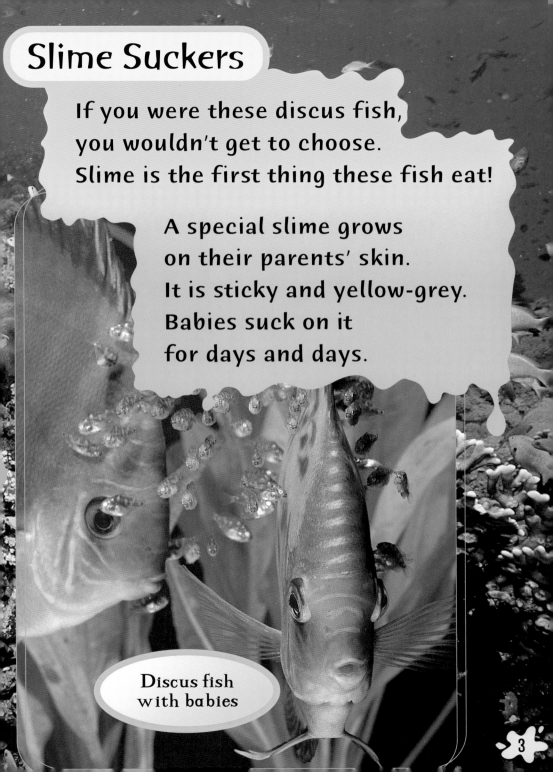

Slime Suckers

If you were these discus fish,
you wouldn't get to choose.
Slime is the first thing these fish eat!

A special slime grows
on their parents' skin.
It is sticky and yellow-grey.
Babies suck on it
for days and days.

Discus fish
with babies

3

Slime Movers

Slugs and snails move with slime! They glide along on a layer of slime that oozes out from under their body.

A snail has just one foot. It moves in waves over slime.

4

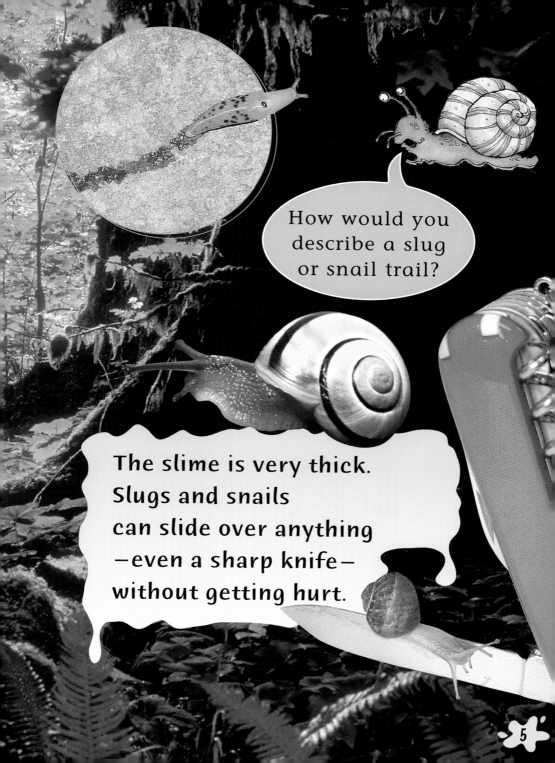

How would you describe a slug or snail trail?

The slime is very thick. Slugs and snails can slide over anything —even a sharp knife— without getting hurt.

Slime Fighters

Slime may look soft and gooey,
but don't be fooled.
It can be dangerous, too!
When some termites see danger,
they shoot poison slime
out of their heads!

Termite mound

You can see
the poisonous slime
coming out of this
soldier termite.

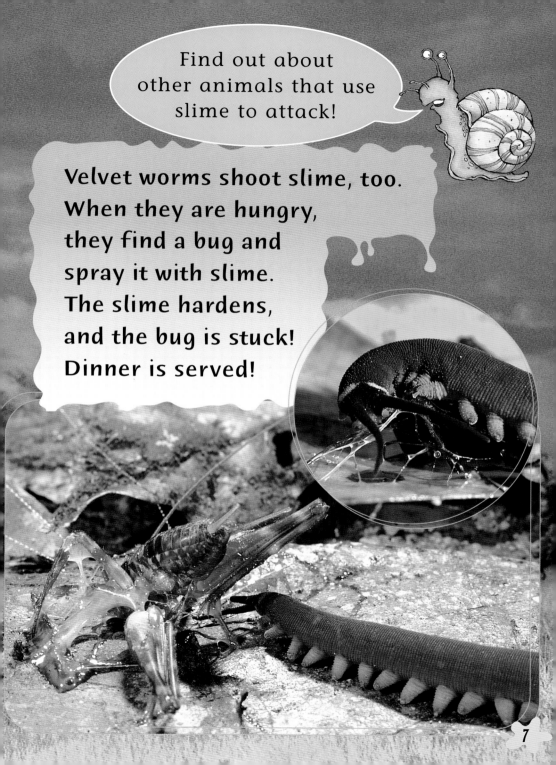

Find out about other animals that use slime to attack!

Velvet worms shoot slime, too. When they are hungry, they find a bug and spray it with slime. The slime hardens, and the bug is stuck! Dinner is served!

7

Slime Sleepers

Lungfish sleep in slime!
If the water in which
they live dries up,
a slimy bed helps them
stay alive.

First they dig a long hole in the mud.
Then they coat the walls with slime.
Outside, the mud hole hardens.
The fish stay in their holes
for up to four years,
until it rains again.

Slime and You

Slime may be gross, but it comes in handy for many animals— even you!

Just think about your nose when you've got a cold or your mouth when you eat! You make slime, too!

SLIME SCIENCE

Written by Laura Hirschfield
Photographed by Susanna Burton

You will need:

1 bowl

½ cup white glue

1 ½ cups warm water

1 tablespoon borax

Food colouring (any colour)

Step 1

Put a few drops
of food colouring
and ½ cup
of warm water
into a bowl.
Add ½ cup
of glue and mix.

Step 2

Ask an adult to help you
with this step.
Put the borax in one cup
of warm water.
Stir until the powder
dissolves.

Step 3

Add the borax mixture
to the glue mixture,
a little bit at a time.
Stir gently.
Now you've got slime!

Now it's time to experiment with your slime.

Slime Stretch

Take some slime
and pull on it.
How far will it stretch?
Use a ruler to measure
how far it goes.

Now hold the slime
and let it hang down.
How far will it stretch?
Measure it.
Which way stretches more?
Why do you think this is?

For each experiment,
write down your guess
and then write down
what happens.

Slime Fold

Press some slime into a pancake shape. How many times can you fold it?

Slime Time

Put two balls of slime on a table or desk. Will they touch each other? How long might it take?

Slime Balls and Worms

Roll some slime into balls and worms.
Put them on a table or desk.
What do you think will happen?

What other experiments could you try?

Slugger and Me

Written by Milo & Mason   Illustrated by Ian Forss

When I was ten,
I went to live with Aunt Peach.
Aunt Peach was a normal person,
except for one thing.
Aunt Peach liked slugs.

She liked slugs so much
that she raised them.
She raised award-winning slugs.
And her pride and joy was Slugger.

Aunt Peach treated Slugger
better than she treated me.
She'd talk to him, saying,
"How's my sweet little Slugger today?"

She even stroked him with her finger.
"Everybody needs love," said Aunt Peach.

"Gross!" I said.

Aunt Peach never told Slugger what to do.
But she was always telling me
to turn off the TV and do stuff.
"Do this," she'd say. "Do that."

I'd say, "Right after this cartoon."
Then she'd start talking to Slugger
and forget.

When she'd remember, she'd say,
"Didn't I tell you to do something?"

I'd say, "Oh, yeah. Right after this cartoon."
That way, I never had to do anything.

One day, Aunt Peach said that
Slugger needed exercise.
She asked me to race him
across the rug.

"Right after this cartoon," I said.

Then Aunt Peach said,
"If you beat Slugger,
I'll never tell you to do anything again.
If you lose, you have to do what I ask."

I couldn't believe my luck.
This was going to be a cinch!
"Deal!" I said.

Aunt Peach got Slugger.
We took our places.

"Ready, set, go!"

Slugger didn't move.
I didn't either.
What was the hurry?
Besides, I wanted to watch
my favourite programme.

When the programme was over,
Slugger had barely moved.
So I watched another programme,
and another, until I fell asleep.

When I woke, a trail of slime
went right across the rug.

Oh no!
Slugger was oozing over the finish line!

"Slugger won!" cried Aunt Peach.

Now I'm Aunt Peach's slave.
You won't believe all the stuff
she makes me do.

She makes me brush my teeth.
She makes me shower.
She makes me do my homework.
Once, Aunt Peach even made me
take out the rubbish!
Gross!

My life is ruined.
Now I've hardly got time for TV!
I've changed my mind about slugs.
I mean, slugs don't have to do anything.
Slugs have got it made.

The Hagfish

Slime of the Sea

Written by Linda Johns

Illustrated by Leonardo Meschini and Fraser Williamson

Meet the hagfish.
Slime is its life.

The hagfish lives
deep in the sea.
It has no bones.
It looks like a big worm.

The hagfish makes its own slime.
Slime comes out of its nose.
Slime comes out of its sides.
It makes gobs and gobs of goo.

AAACHOOO!
A hagfish sneezes to get
all the slime out of
its nose.

Don't scare a hagfish!
Why?
It will slime you!

When a hagfish is scared,
it makes extra slime.
The slime helps it slip away.
It gets away fast!

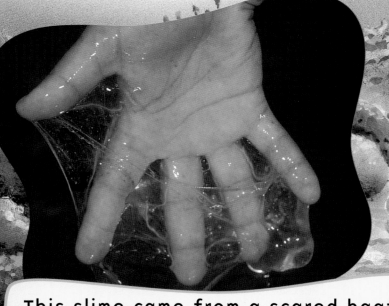

This slime came from a scared hagfish.
The hagfish can make
a bucket of slime in a minute.
Then, if you give it a moment,
it can do it all over again!

Even a hagfish needs to clean up.
It ties itself in a knot
to get rid of its slime.

The hagfish
ties itself into a knot
that moves up its body.
As the knot moves,
it pushes off
the slime.

Lunchtime means more slime.
A hagfish eats worms and dead fish.
This helps to clean up the sea.
It is so slimy that
it can slip inside
a dead fish.
It eats the fish
from the inside out!

Will sir be dining in again?

Scientists say the hagfish is old
and, when they say old,
they mean really old.

The hagfish has been swimming
in the sea for millions of years.
It may be slimy,
but it knows how to survive.

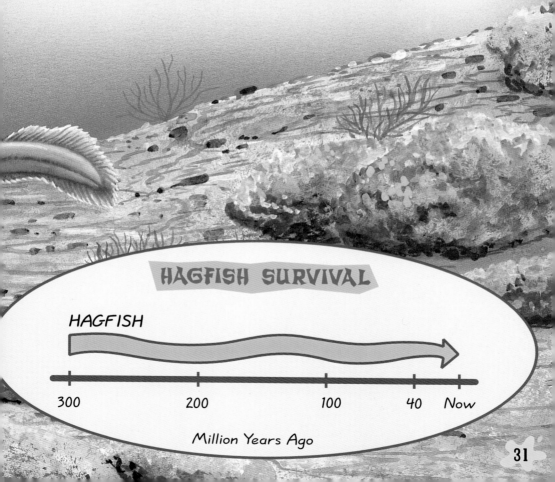

HAGFISH SURVIVAL

HAGFISH

300   200   100   40   Now

Million Years Ago

Index